MW01241793

THE
WINE
OF THE
KINGDOM

Steve Slater

THE WINE OF THE KINGDOM
©2019 by Steve Slater

Unless otherwise noted, Scripture quotations are from the ESV® Bible (The Holy Bible, English Standard Version®), copyright © 2001 by Crossway, a publishing ministry of Good News Publishers. Used by permission. All rights reserved.

ISBN: 978-1-66782-073-6

Thump Keg Publishing
1630 W Ridge St
Wytheville VA 24382-1527

To purchase: ThumpKegPublishing.com
To contact the author: thumpkeg@icloud.com

ACKNOWLEDGEMENTS

"'How is it that this man has learning, when he has never studied?' So Jesus answered them, 'My teaching is not mine, but his who sent me…"[1]

These pages do not reflect any creativity on my part, but rather an attempt to put on paper my observations from the Bible about the kingdom of God. I'm not a theologian in the academic sense, nor a credentialed Bible scholar. The reader can and should examine the cited biblical texts himself to evaluate how they have been interpreted and applied.

Many of the kingdom principles in this booklet were brought to my attention by Dr. John Ridgway. Some of them were highlighted during a trip we took together to Central Asia. I wrote down these pages immediately after that trip.

Bill Swan has been an ongoing influence by his input and example over many years since we were students together at Virginia Tech. Searching out the Scriptures with integrity, he has labored long to see an unencumbered gospel penetrate the soil of Japan. The principles he modeled there embody the kingdom perspective I have tried to highlight here.

---

1. John 7:15-16

THE WINE OF THE KINGDOM

Introduction

Many of us have never experienced living in a kingdom. In the U.S. we tend not to like kings. But try to imagine an Israeli who lived in the glorious days of Solomon, when his country was highly regarded among the nations during a time of peace and great prosperity. They were the people of the true creator God, a light among the nations. What was it like to then see the temple destroyed, to go into exile, to be subject to a foreign king, to suffer many years of humiliation under one empire after another—Babylonian, Greek, Persian, Roman?

Of course, other nations have fallen from greatness. Hitler exploited Germany's humiliation resulting from defeat in World War I. He appealed to their identity as the master race and called them to be great again. In Russia and America, politicians have spoken of restoring our countries to greatness. Similarly the Jews must have longed for the day when the Messiah would restore Israel to its former glory.

The Kingdom is Like...

Jesus's message that the kingdom of God was near likely struck a deep chord that resonated within the Jewish population. They were looking forward to a real king and a literal kingdom. They were not mistaken in their anticipation. Jesus *was* their real king, the heir to David's throne. His kingdom also was a real kingdom.

How that kingdom was to be established and expand, however, was absolutely unexpected. Consequently, Jesus constantly taught about the nature of the kingdom. He clarified with many illustrations. "The kingdom of God is like..." In actuality King Jesus's reign was established under the noses of then existing world rulers, and it continues to expand today![2]

Ignoring Jesus's Teaching about the Kingdom

Jesus began His ministry by announcing that the kingdom of God is at hand.[3] Certainly there is a future aspect to the coming of God's kingdom.[4] However, Jesus already has broken into history and inaugurated His kingdom. He went about teaching the good news of the kingdom.[5]

Initially it was difficult for me to get a handle on this concept. I had heard few sermons about the kingdom of God. I vaguely associated it with going to heaven and the afterlife. Although it clearly was the focus of Jesus's teaching, my perspective was framed more by unconscious religious memes than by what Jesus said.

Down to the present day, Jesus's words about the kingdom often seem to get overlooked in favor of a more practical, organizational emphasis. When taken seriously, Jesus's teaching on the kingdom presents an embarrassing contradiction to traditional practices in church history. One interpretation that attempts to address this incongruity is the view that because the Jews rejected Jesus, the kingdom was delayed and the "church age" introduced in its place. As a result the "kingdom age" is not viewed as relevant to the present, but relegated to a not-so-near future.

———————————

2. Ps. 2; Isa. 9:6-7

3. Mark 1:15

4. Luke 21:31; 11:2

5. Luke 4:43; 8:1; 16:16; 17:20-21

In contrast to Jesus's focus on the kingdom, sermons about attendance, tithing, membership, building programs, and similar topics have not been lacking. Progress in any of these areas can provide an appearance of success and a sense of accomplishment. Yet these topics are only the containers, not the wine itself.

Confusing the Wine with the Wineskins

We encounter the story of the wine and the wineskins in chapter 2 of Mark's gospel. This chapter records a series of actions by Jesus, which were controversial in the eyes of the religious elite. He breaks their rules, violates scruples, and creates theological dilemmas. He associates with unsavory people. He disregards conventions about Sabbath observance. He doesn't observe their religious traditions. He forgives sins.

When questioned about neglecting the observance of fasts, Jesus replies that at the present time fasting is not appropriate. Evidently fasting is valuable when it serves a purpose, but not as an end in itself. Similarly, he replies that associating with "sinners" served a vital purpose. Rules, external forms and practices can serve a helpful spiritual purpose, but they are not an end in themselves. They were not intended to be served, but to serve. Jesus says that the Sabbath was intended to serve man, not for man to serve the Sabbath.

The wineskins are the externals, but the wine itself is spiritual. The kingdom of God is not defined by geography, race, physical markers, earthly structures or organizations -- but it can penetrate them! When penetrated, they become physical, visible, external containers of the wine. The kingdom itself exists wherever Christ the King rules in the hearts of men – God's will on earth as it is in heaven.

The old wineskins of Jewish practices served a valid function, but the kingdom which was drawing near would render them obsolete. And the gospel of the kingdom could not be confined within them without itself becoming compromised, distorted or lost.

Mistaking the wineskins of religion for the wine of the kingdom can be a major impediment to the expansion of the gospel into other cultures. Wineskins that serve believers in their own culture may not be helpful in a different culture. Imposing extra-biblical church forms and viewing various religious practices as essential attach a yoke of cultural baggage to our message that distorts the gospel. The book of Galatians, for example, addresses the distortion of the gospel which occurred when Jewish Christians insisted that Gentile converts follow Jewish practices.

Wineskins and Church

Jesus said that *he* would build his church and that it would be built on the foundation of those who by the Holy Spirit recognized that he was the Son of God and Christ.[6] "Christ" means God's anointed or Messiah, King. Jesus, the King, spoke much about a kingdom.

Jesus often speaks of how the children of the kingdom will, not congregate, but penetrate![7] Church is not a meeting. As he told Peter in the verse just cited, the gates of hell would not prevail against his church. Some imagine Jesus's words as describing hell attacking the church, but when did gates ever attack anything? Jesus does not envision a fortress. Quite the opposite. It is hell that is playing defense, because gates are

6. Matt. 16:15-18. See also 1 Cor. 12:3.

7. Matt. 13:38; Luke 13:20-21

THE WINE OF THE KINGDOM

defensive. Jesus's church will batter down the gates of hell. Church is mounting the assault, which is breaking down hell's defenses and freeing its prisoners.

Church is neither a place, nor something we do. Church is who we are. It is people who, by the work of the Holy Spirit, have recognized that Jesus is King. Much like Peter and the early apostles, we may be surprised to discover that there are those far from our cultural and religious practices who have received the Holy Spirit and follow Jesus as Lord and King.

Bloom Where You are Planted

In 1 Corinthians 7, Paul sets out a principle that he follows in all the churches:

> On*ly let each person lead the life that the Lord has assigned to him, and to which God has called him.* This is my rule in all the churches. Was anyone at the time of his call already circumcised? Let him not seek to remove the marks of circumcision. Was anyone at the time of his call uncircumcised? Let him not seek circumcision. *Each one should remain in the condition in which he was called.* Were you a bondservant when called? Do not be concerned about it. (But if you can gain your freedom, avail yourself of the opportunity.) .... *So, brothers, in whatever condition each was called, there let him remain with God* [emphases added]. [8]

Some things are determined by our first birth, such as race, family, economic status, background, innate talents, appearance, physical abilities, disabilities, and limitations.

---

8. 1 Cor. 7:17-24

8

According to Paul, these factors play a role in our calling. They are not happenstance, but God ordained. As Paul indicates, if changing our economic or social status is an option, great! Otherwise, we are to embrace the circumstances of our first birth as our calling. Paul even includes religious identity. Gentiles should not convert to Judaism, nor vice versa. In some countries religion is legally determined by birth. In some places, formal religious choice is not an option.

Honoring the first birth facilitates the receptiveness, understanding, and transmission of the gospel within a culture. Ignoring or denigrating the aspects of first birth can introduce unnecessary obstacles to the gospel and its mobility.

It is significant that the gospel was not encumbered by exporting Jewish wineskins to the Gentiles! Discarding the God-given requirements of Jewish law was not a simple matter for Peter, raised in them from childhood. God revealed to him in a vision that recurred three times that he must not call unclean what God now declares clean (for Peter, now indwelt by the Holy Spirit, the protective wall of Jewish regulations has been removed). Peter is free to visit and associate with the "unclean" Roman centurion Cornelius on his home turf.[9]

Peter did not invite newly converted Cornelius to attend meetings in Jerusalem. No synagogues or meeting halls were erected. Instead, the gospel invaded Cornelius's world—his family, his extended household, his friends, other Roman soldiers, and his acquaintances in the Gentile world. People remained in their natural settings and relationships. Gentiles were not extracted from their existing ties to attend meetings

---

9. Acts 10

with Jewish strangers Throughout the New Testament we see the phrase "the church in your household."[10]

Today there are movements to Christ in all nine branches of Islam where followers of Christ remain in their communities and in their Muslim cultural identity. Over five million Muslims have become followers of Christ in one country alone. Even when considered "bad Muslims," they are still viewed as part of their community. They are able to live out the gospel with changed lives among family and friends in their natural relationships. Similar movements are taking place throughout the world in Hindu, Buddhist, Shinto, and other religious communities.

It is often more costly to remain in one's religious context than to relocate to a western church or to another country. Some even risk death by following Paul's "rule in all the churches" to remain where called. They understand that staying connected enables the spread of the gospel.

As one retains ties within his native religion, of course, questions of conscience may arise. Such was the norm with many first century Gentile converts. The book of 1 Corinthians addresses these kinds of issues. In it Paul lays out practical guidelines for how followers of Christ can continue to remain and associate, yet not participate, in certain practices, such as the worship of idols.

---

10. Some translations: "the church *that meets* in your household"; however, *meet* is not in the Greek text. (Philem. 2; Rom. 16:5; 1 Cor. 16:19; Col. 4:15)

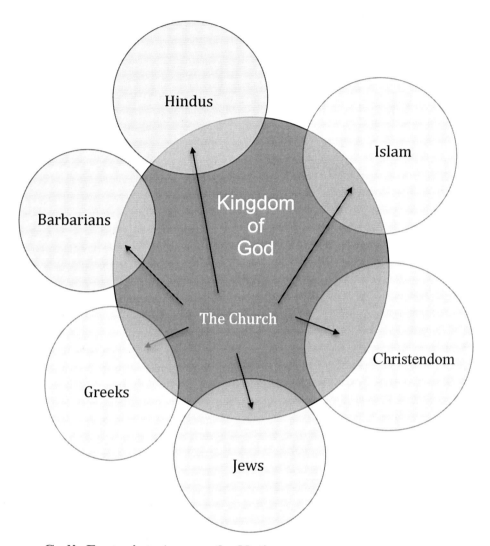

God's Footprints Among the Nations

The Scriptures indicate that God has a unique history in each nation of bringing every nation to a true or truer knowledge of the creator God.

> ...He made from one man every nation of mankind to live on all the face of the earth, having determined allotted periods and the boundaries of their dwelling

place, that they should seek God, and perhaps feel their way toward him and find him. Yet he is actually not far from each one of us, for "in him we live and move and have our being";' as even some of your own poets have said, "For we are indeed his offspring." Being then God's offspring, we ought not to think that the divine being is like gold or silver or stone, an image formed by the art and imagination of man. The times of ignorance God overlooked, but now he commands all people everywhere to repent, because he has fixed a day on which he will judge the world in righteousness by a man whom he has appointed; and of this he has given assurance to all by raising him from the dead.[11]

Though grieved over the idolatry he saw in Athens, Paul did not rebuke them. He commended them for being religious! He quoted their native poets. When we connect with the witness God has left in another culture, we can discover pathways for the gospel. Just as John the Baptist prepared the ground for Jesus and was a light in the Jewish culture, there are voices and truths in other cultures and religions that we can affirm. To tell someone that everything he senses about God is wrong because it does not come in a Christianized package can be to trample on the precious glimpses of light from God he has experienced in a dark world.

Rather than categorically view all religions as competitors, we sometimes discover them to be stepping stones to Christ, a tutor like the law was for Jews. Jesus did not squelch a flickering candle. He affirmed truth and examples of faith when he saw it, saying "you are not far from the kingdom of God." The gospels record a number of examples where he

---

11. Acts 7:26-31

valued in others what some religious leaders overlooked or even disdained. He often singled out those who were not Jewish as examples of exemplary faith in his parables.

Journalist John Gunther (*Inside Europe, Inside Asia, Inside Africa*, et al) documented in ancient cultures which he explored old traditions of a supreme Creator. Polytheism arose later. The memory of a creator God existed even among isolated Polynesian island peoples. Over generations a preoccupation with idolatrous gods of war and sex and popular folk religions supplanted, but never completely erased, the awareness of a holy Creator.

> For his invisible attributes, namely, his eternal power and divine nature, have been clearly perceived, ever since the creation of the world, in the things that have been made. So they are without excuse. For although they knew God, they did not honor him as God or give thanks to him, but they became futile in their thinking, and their foolish hearts were darkened. Claiming to be wise, they became fools, and exchanged the glory of the immortal God for images resembling mortal man and birds and animals and creeping things.[12]

Descendants of Abraham

Three world religions have preserved the knowledge of the true creator God from degrading into idolatry. Christianity, Judaism, and Islam all have their origin in the promises God gave the descendants of Abraham. Even though God chose the descendants of Abraham through Isaac as His special inheritance, he also promised Abraham blessing upon those descendants who would comprise the nations of Islam:

12. Rom. 1:20-23

As for Ishmael, I have heard you; behold, I have
blessed him and will make him fruitful and multiply
him greatly. He shall father twelve princes, and I will
make him into a great nation. But I will establish my
covenant with Isaac...[13]

All Nations Inherit God's Blessing to Abraham

God's promise to bless all the families of the earth through
Abraham's descendant[14] was to come through the lineage of
his son Isaac, whose son was Jacob, the father of the twelve
tribes of Israel. In Isaiah 5 God describes Israel as a carefully
cultivated vine. Because the vine did not bear fruit, God
warned that it could be cut down. Seven hundred years later
John the Baptist also warned: "And do not presume to say to
yourselves, 'We have Abraham as our father,' for I tell you,
God is able from these stones to raise up children for Abraham.
Even now the axe is laid to the root of the trees."[15]

Indeed, God raised up children of Abraham apart from
his physical descendants. The knowledge of the true God, the
revelations, the prophets, the Bible, the commandments, the
promises, the Messiah – all the rich heritage of the Jews was
inherited by all the nations through faith in Christ.

Now I am speaking to you Gentiles. Inasmuch then as I
am an apostle to the Gentiles... if some of the branches
were broken off, and you, although a wild olive shoot,
were grafted in among the others and now share in the

---

13. Gen. 17:20

14. Gen. 12:3; 18:18; 22:18; 26:14; 28:14

15. Matt. 3:9

nourishing root of the olive tree, do not be arrogant toward the branches. If you are, remember it is not you who support the root, but the root that supports you.[16]

The inclusion of the Gentiles was made possible by the death of Christ on the cross, the one through whom God promised Abraham all the families of the earth would be blessed.

Now among those who went up to worship at the feast were some Greeks. So these came to Philip, who was from Bethsaida in Galilee, and asked him, "Sir, we wish to see Jesus." Philip went and told Andrew; Andrew and Philip went and told Jesus. And Jesus answered them, "The hour has come for the Son of Man to be glorified. Truly, truly, I say to you, unless a grain of wheat falls into the earth and dies, it remains alone; but if it dies, it bears much fruit."[17]

Wall of Separation Is Removed

The Jewish people were distinguished from the other nations by the law given through Moses. It was a wall of protection from the extreme moral degradation of the surrounding tribes. Observing the commandments would keep them from the diseases, bloodshed, oppression, famines, and perversions that afflicted others. They would preserve in the world the truth about God from the influence of idolatry. They were blessed if they kept the law of God. If they did not keep the law they would be cursed with all these things and more. The law's benefit was dependent upon human moral effort and goodness, love of God and man.

---

16. Rom. 11:18-13

17. John 12:20-24

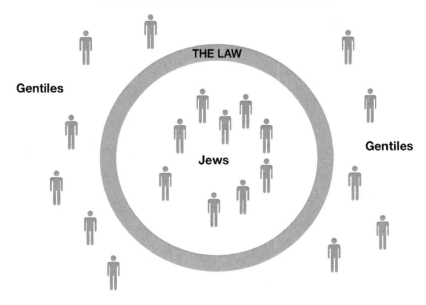

The law was good and holy. Unfortunately, people were not, and that was a problem. The blessing of the law was dependent upon keeping it. Not keeping it entailed a curse. They possessed, knew, and taught the law, but they did not keep it. They law meant for blessing became a curse.

Other nations without the law, but in possession of a moral conscience, were also separated from God and without any real hope.[18] All mankind stood condemned by their moral choices. Thus, only because of what transpired on the cross were both Jews and Gentiles, both those far from God and those near to God, given access to a holy God.

> Therefore remember that at one time you Gentiles in the flesh, called "the uncircumcision" by what is called the circumcision, which is made in the flesh by hands— remember that you were at that time separated from Christ, alienated from the commonwealth of Israel and strangers to the covenants of promise, having no hope

18. Rom. 2:14-15

and without God in the world. But now in Christ Jesus you who once were far off have been brought near by the blood of Christ. For he himself is our peace, who has made us both one and has broken down in his flesh the dividing wall of hostility by abolishing the law of commandments expressed in ordinances, that he might create in himself one new man in place of the two, so making peace, and might reconcile us both to God in one body through the cross, thereby killing the hostility. And he came and preached peace to you who were far off and peace to those who were near. For through him we both have access in one Spirit to the Father. So then you are no longer strangers and aliens, but you are fellow citizens with the saints and members of the household of God.[19]

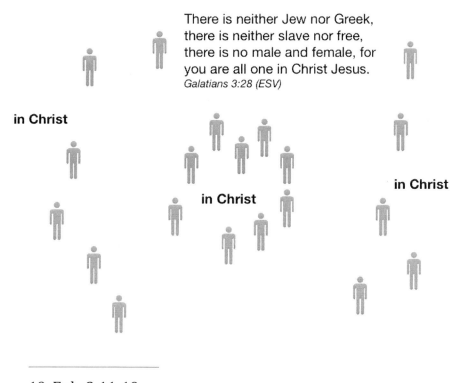

There is neither Jew nor Greek, there is neither slave nor free, there is no male and female, for you are all one in Christ Jesus.
Galatians 3:28 (ESV)

in Christ

in Christ

in Christ

---

19. Eph. 2:11-19

Ultimately, the way of blessing was not through the law but through the sacrifice of Christ. In abolishing the law, which defined Jews in contrast to Gentiles, God obviously did not erect a new set of external rules and commandments. Yet, a new legal system has been instituted if the gospel of the kingdom becomes replaced by a Christian religion of rules!

How could God dare to remove the protective fence of regulations he had given through Moses? How can we today have a church without clear external rules and controls? These understandable concerns have been voiced by defenders of various legalistic institutions throughout church history.

The Essential Reality of the Holy Spirit

Since Pentecost God has "poured out the Holy Spirit on all flesh."[20] Not only prophets or anointed leaders, but now every believer has been made a partaker of God's own nature. The law was internalized, written on the heart. The external protective fence of the law could be removed. Consequently, there is no longer any distinction between Jew and Gentile, since all come to God only through Christ without regard to the law or any other human efforts, practices or qualifications.

> There is neither Jew nor Greek, there is neither slave nor free, there is no male and female, for you are all one in Christ Jesus. And if you are Christ's, then you are Abraham's offspring, heirs according to promise[21]

---

20. Acts 2:17

21. Gal. 3:28-29

18

The Implications

In Acts 15 the apostles "astonished that the Holy Spirit was poured out even upon the Gentiles" concluded that Gentiles were free from the requirements of the law of Moses, such as circumcision or the observance of religious holidays and ceremonies. Paul writes that believers should embrace the circumstances into which they were born as their personal calling from God. If born Jewish they should remain Jewish. If Gentile, they should remain Gentile, etc. When we teach (consciously or unconsciously) that someone from another background must become Christian in a cultural sense, we violate this principle, distort the gospel, and hinder its advance. Customs accumulated over centuries of church history (not necessarily bad) are not biblically synonymous with church or the kingdom of God.

The Kingdom is Spiritual

The external markers, the rules and regulations that define Judaism or Christian religious practice are a shadow of the reality in Christ. They may be helpful to some, but they are not the essentials when the reality has come. Let's examine some of these wineskins.

Water Baptism

The Jewish apostles baptized both Jewish and Gentile converts with water, at least some of the time, since water baptism was a familiar rite in the Jewish world.[22] It is noteworthy that Peter, in speaking of water baptism, wrote that he did not have in mind a mere ceremony with water but an appeal to God.[23] Consider what Ananias said to Paul at his

---

22. Heb. 6:2

23. 1 Pet. 3:21

conversion: "And now why do you wait? Rise and be baptized and wash away your sins, calling on his name."[24] Like Peter, Ananias implies an appeal to God. In today's evangelical world other forms of an appeal have evolved, such as "going forward" or the "sinner's prayer." Few would maintain that such outward forms in themselves are the point. The appeal to God is the point.

What about the Lord's command in Matthew 28:19-20? The word *baptize* is a transliteration of a non-religious word in common use by a Greek speaker of that day. *Baptism* connoted "immersion into" something. The earliest translations of Matthew 28:19-20 (Egyptian and Syriac) render the Greek in just such language—immersion *into* God the Father, the Son, and the Holy Spirit. Cambridge scholar F. H. Chase writes: "What if we...instead of transliterating it, venture to translate it... surely a Greek-speaking Christian would understand the words. He would regard the divine Name as the element, so to speak, into which the baptized is plunged."[25]

The original Greek of Matthew 28:19-20 then is quite clear. Jesus is saying that by making disciples and teaching them to observe all that he commands, one is immersing them into God (not water). John the Baptist, the last of the Old Testament prophets said, "I immerse you into water, but he [Christ] will immerse you into the Holy Spirit."[26]

---

24. Acts 22:16

25. F. H. Chase, "The Lord's Command to Baptize" in *The Journal of Theological Studies* (Oxford University Press, 1905), vol. 6, pp. 481-512

26. translating (vs. transliterating) the Greek in Mark 1:8

In Corinth where rivalries arose, Paul said he was glad he had not baptized most of them lest they identify with him. He went so far as to say that Christ did not send him to baptize, but to preach the gospel of Christ.[27] It seems Paul is referring to the external Jewish rite of water baptism and did not consider it an essential. Jesus Christ himself did not baptize anyone with water.[28]

Whatever the position on water baptism, and there are many positions, the external *form* of water baptism (the form itself, apart from an appeal to God) appears to be a wineskin.

Sanctuary, House of Worship, Church

The law described how to worship and where to worship—at the temple in Jerusalem. Yet Jesus replied to the Samaritan woman, "Woman, believe me, the hour is coming when neither on this mountain nor in Jerusalem will you worship the Father...the hour is coming, and is now here, when the true worshipers will worship the Father in spirit and truth."[29] Since the third century the church building has held a central place in Christendom, but Paul and Peter describe the temple that God is building as the believers themselves.[30]

Worship

The Jews associated worship with temple sacrifice. Paul now describes worship in a spiritual sense as presenting

---

27. 1 Cor. 1:17

28. John 4:2

29. John 4:20-23

30. Eph. 2:19-21; 1 Pet. 2:5

yourself as a living sacrifice. In the full context of this passage, he is saying that worship is living a transformed life 24/7.[31]

Early believers gathered together, but they did not gather to worship. They met to interact. They did worship, but all other aspects of everyday life were also worship. Historian Robert Banks writes:

> Since all places and times have now become the venue for worship, Paul cannot speak of Christians assembling in church distinctively for this purpose. They are already worshiping God, acceptably or unacceptably, in whatever they are doing. While this means that when they are in church they are worshiping as well, it is not worship but something else that marks off their coming together from everything else that they are doing.[32]

Sunday
The kingdom is every day. Setting aside a special day may be beneficial, but it is not essential. "One person esteems one day as better than another, while another esteems all days alike. Each one should be fully convinced in his own mind."[33]

Pastor, Priest
Christ warned us that our leadership model should not resemble the world's.[34] In the Body of Christ, there is only one

---

31. Rom. 12:1,2

32. Robert Banks, *Paul's Idea of Community: The Early House Churches in their Historical Setting* (Exeter 1980), p. 91f.

33. Rom. 14:5

34. Matt. 20:25-28

head. Jesus Christ is not merely a figurehead—someone to whom we pray a perfunctory prayer before a meeting. He is alive, not a mute idol.[35] He speaks through the various gifts of the indwelling Holy Spirit. His leadership occurs as each believer functions in the area of his spiritual enabling. We assert ourselves when a need occurs in our area of gifting and defer to others when the situation coincides with their gifting.[36]

A pastor fulfills his role as he seeks to build dependence upon Christ, not himself. In fact, all gifts strengthen others in their own gifting and connection to Christ as we build up another. Hierarchal titles and positions may have their place in Christian organizations of various kinds, but they do not reflect the spiritual dynamic within the Body of Christ.[37]

We can see that many religious and cultural wineskins have their counterparts in the kingdom of God. These external markers are shadows of spiritual realities in the kingdom of God. "In him also you were circumcised with a circumcision made without hands, by putting off the body of the flesh, by the circumcision of Christ."[38]

The following chart, which may not be accurate in every detail for every culture and denomination, is only intended to help illustrate the distinction between the wine of the kingdom and the wineskins that are shadows or reflections (icons) of kingdom realities.

---

35. 1 Cor. 12:2

36. 1 Cor. 12

37. Matt. 23:8-11

38. Col. 2:11

Wineskins in Judaism	Wineskins in Christendom	Realities in Kingdom of God
circumcision	water baptism	Holy Spirit baptism
temple	church building	believers
sacrifices	worship service	transformed lives
Sabbath	Sunday	24/7
priesthood	pastor/priest	Jesus Christ

"Therefore do not let anyone judge you by what you eat or drink, or with regard to a religious festival, a New Moon celebration or a Sabbath day. These are a shadow of the things that were to come; the reality, however, is found in Christ."[39]

The Kingdom is Relational

Have you ever been part of a group, maybe at a social function or church meeting and felt that no one really knew you? You may have felt self-conscious and uncomfortable. We have a desire to be known. I believe God also desires to be known. He wants to reveal to us his thoughts, his ways. God seeks relationship. Jesus defined eternal life as knowing God and Christ.[40] Jesus said the two greatest commands were to love God with all of our being, and to love our neighbors as ourselves. You can give all you have to the poor and not have love.[41] Love implies relationship.

Jesus is described as the word of God become flesh living among us. We beheld His glory, John writes, full of

---

39. Col. 2:16-17 (NIV); see also Heb. 8:5; 10:1

40. John 17:3

41. 1 Cor. 13:3

grace and truth.[42] When John describes his experience, it is not an academic concept. He writes, "That which was from the beginning, which we have heard, which we have seen with our eyes, which we looked upon and have touched with our hands… that which we have seen and heard we proclaim also to you, so that you too may have fellowship with us; and indeed our fellowship is with the Father and with his Son Jesus Christ."[43] God sent His message in the form of a human life.

"More is caught than taught" is an old adage. Developments in neurology indicate that life change seldom comes from understanding truths with the conceptualizing part of the brain. Change happens when truth is felt—for example, when experienced in a relationship. Jesus was the Word incarnate that people experienced and felt. He *was* the gospel. *We also are the gospel!* Our life is a letter that God is writing to others.[44] Jesus even said that we are the light of the world![45]

We may not feel up to such a lofty description because we are flawed. We mess up. "We have this treasure in jars of clay."[46] The message is not about us, but about the One who indwells us. If we are vulnerable and do not hide our true selves, including our flaws and struggles, others will not mistake us as the source of light. The light shines brightest when we are authentic, and our lives are open and accessible. Walking in the light is not about sinlessness, but about not

---

42. paraphrase of John 1:14

43. John 1:14, 1 John 1:1-3

44. 2 Cor. 3:3

45. Matt. 5:14

46. 2 Cor. 4:5-7

deceiving ourselves or others. No pretense. No hypocrisy. Consider 1 John 1:7-9:

> But if we walk in the light, as he is in the light, we have fellowship with one another, and the blood of Jesus his Son cleanses us from all sin. If we say we have no sin, we deceive ourselves, and the truth is not in us. If we confess our sins, he is faithful and just to forgive us our sins and to cleanse us from all unrighteousness.

Others may find encouragement that we are all very much alike in our human weaknesses and see our message as accessible to them in their own difficult circumstances.

Jesus prays for us to be in the world and at the same time to be kept from the evil in the world.[47] Being in the world is a matter of cultivating our natural relationships: initiating friendships with the people around us, joining a civic club, getting involved in the local community, valuing extended family members, repairing difficult relationships, being available to serve relatives in time of need, and so on.

Apart from these broader relationships, the special relational bonds among believers are the essence of church.[48] As we serve one another in the diverse ways that the Holy Spirit enables each of us, we grow into a fuller knowledge (experience) of Christ. The gifts listed in the New Testament describe the various examples of how the Holy Spirit enables us to relate and serve one another. Beware of reading into these functions hierarchal titles. The influence of each believer is based on the authority of truth, integrity and God's Word.

---

47. John 17

48. Eph. 4:11-16; Col. 2:19

There may be value in organization wineskins, but the dynamic of the kingdom is relational and spiritual.

The Value of a Kingdom Perspective

Jesus said, "Do not judge by appearances, but judge with right judgment."[49] The spiritually immature judge by the external. We can subtly, or not so subtly, find our security in those things which are external, visible, and quantifiable.

The wine of the kingdom is mysterious. Its advance can seem insignificant. There were the large crowds that Jesus did not commit to. There was the handful of unlikely, uneducated, unimpressive, and quite imperfect men he did commit to. Rejection, desertion and a humiliating death concludes His earthly ministry. A tiny, obscure mustard seed that becomes a great tree of shelter for many—this is a trait of the kingdom.[50]

Of the seven churches Jesus evaluated in the book of Revelation, only two were praised without censure. To the church at Smyrna, Jesus said, "I know your tribulation and your poverty (but you are rich)… Be faithful unto death, and I will give you the crown of life." He said to the church at Philadelphia, "I know that you have but little power, and yet you have kept my word and have not denied my name." On the other hand, He said to the church at Sardis, "I know your works. You have the reputation of being alive, but you are dead." And to the church at Laodicea, He said, "For you say, I am rich, I have prospered, and I need nothing, not realizing that you are wretched, pitiable, poor, blind, and naked." [51]

---

49. John 7:24

50. Mark 4:30-32

51. Rev. 2-3

Focusing on wineskins inevitably results in an appraisal at odds with that which Jesus gave. Poor judgment is the tragic consequence of looking through institutional lenses. It leads to bad decisions by seeking growth at the expense of true kingdom advance.

A kingdom perspective informs our priorities, our discernment, our values, and all that we do. Organizations, like individuals, must die to self-preservation and personal ambition to be able serve the kingdom.[52] Kingdom-focused people think in terms of movement—movement, over which they have no control and for which they receive no credit. They pursue alignment with the King, rather than self-promotion. Seeking first the kingdom, all else follows.[53]

For Further Reading

Ridgway, John. *Your Kingdom Come.* NavGrads International, 2018

---

52. John 12:24

53. Matt. 6:33

Form and Function

Wine and wineskins can be seen as a metaphor for form and function. Consider the function of prayer. At an early age my parents taught me to pray. At bedtime I learned to close my eyes and bow my head as I prayed. In the Bible we find other forms of prayer, such kneeling, lifting up hands toward heaven, or falling prostrate. There is nothing Biblical about closing my eyes and bowing my head. These are FORMS I was taught and how I perform the FUNCTION of prayer.

Sometimes after I go to bed, I remember something I am concerned about. Then I may pray while lying in bed. My intention in distinguishing between form and function (wineskins and wine) is not to denigrate the forms. Forms are unavoidable, but they are not the function itself. Forms should not become sacred cows. Forms that serve a function in one culture can actually hinder the same function in another culture. The function is what is important, as are those forms that facilitate the function. We do not serve the forms. Forms are meant to serve us in carrying out a function.

In a Russian Orthodox Church, there are no pews. Who would dare show such disrespect as to sit in the presence of the tsar? How much more so in the presence of God! A Russian Orthodox friend once told me he could never pray lying in bed! He considered it disrespectful. An Orthodox believer prays standing, kneeling or prostate (unless prevented by special circumstances, such as physical frailty or illness, of course). I myself have no problem sitting while praying, even though sitting may be viewed as disrespect in another culture.

Similarly, my friend's forms can be misunderstood by me and personally uncomfortable. Years ago I recorded my first impressions of a Russian Orthodox service in a letter. The following paragraphs entitled Russian Wineskins are that early letter reproduced here.

Russian Wineskins

According to legend Jesus' disciple Andrew first brought Christianity to Russia. Russia embraced the Orthodox Church around 980 A.D. when Prince Vladimir converted, then baptized his family and then most of the city of Kiev in the Dnieper River. Years later, a successor to his throne, now an Orthodox Christian, voluntarily went to his death rather than raise his hand in violence against the usurpers who sought to overthrow him.

Almost a thousand years later, now in Soviet times, my Moscow friend with whom I had been secretly studying the Bible was excited to sneak me into his church. When he did, I was shocked. The walls and ceiling were covered with paintings. The gold in them and in other objects appeared gaudy to me. There were no pews. People fell prostrate or kneeled on the stone floor in prayer. There were confessions in another part of the room. The Scriptures were being read in yet another corner. There were even baptisms taking place. People were coming and going. A poor elderly lady, thinking I was Russian, unapologetically asked me for money to take a bus home. When I gave her a few rubles more than the fare, she insisted on returning me the extra. Everything was strange and unfamiliar, not what I expected.

Afterwards, my friend enthusiastically asked me my impressions. Since they were negative, I could not answer him directly. Instead I asked him what he thought of when he saw all the gold in the church. (I had thought of material wealth.) He had thought of heaven, that which is tested, refined by fire and endures. I asked about the icon paintings. He was reminded of the "cloud of witnesses" - the saints who had gone before and now surround us and of whom we were a part. I went down my list of negative impressions and discovered that his associations were much different from mine. He took me from icon to icon, using them to explain the Bible and Russia's Christian history to me. My negative reactions had arisen from unfamiliar wineskins, alien to the forms of worship I was raised with.

A few years later I had different impressions when I revisited this church. It was the first time I was allowed a visa to Russia that extended through the Easter holiday. The relationship between the Church and the Soviet state was changing, after a large popular celebration of the millennium of Christianity in Russia. Confiscated monasteries and cathedrals were soon to be returned to the church. My friend had asked me to meet him at his church at 11 p.m. Easter eve. (The Easter service begins at sundown on Saturday and continues all night.) I arrived to find a large circle of police standing around the church. I made my way through the cordon to my friend waiting for me. There was no way to get in through the front, because it was packed with people. He took me to a side door. Because there was no room to squeeze into the crowd of worshippers, he stationed me up front by the altar and disappeared. All became hushed, and I continued to wait. Singing suddenly broke out, bells began to clang, and a midnight procession led by the priests started from the front. As my friend went by, he pulled me into the procession. When I turned around to face the main entrance, I saw before me in the church masses of faces lighted by individual candles. The crowd parted like the Red Sea as we passed through. The doors at the rear of the church swung open, and I saw a sight I will never forget. The church was situated on a hill atop a long flight of stairs. Through the doors I saw a sea of worshippers extending in every direction. With the bells still loudly clanging, the procession circled the church. Many of the policemen still encircling the church crossed themselves as we passed by. Later as I rode the subway home, I saw young people on the train still holding their burning candles. Throughout the day, Russians exchanged greetings with "Christ is risen!" "Christ is risen, indeed!" came the response. A banner stretched across the main street of Moscow read, "Christ is risen!" This Easter event is etched into my memory.

When standing in a Russian Orthodox church, sometimes for hours at a time, I feel that I am getting a glimpse of ancient Russia, intruding into a history of those who have gone before. To be sure, there are many contemporary Russians who have no love for the Orthodox Church. There are many others who feel a deep resonance to the church but have little understanding. I've even heard the comment, "I am an atheist, but I am Orthodox." It is said that to be Russian is to be Orthodox. Even those Russians who profess no sympathy for Orthodoxy have embedded in their thinking a Christian conscience, through their Orthodox culture, music, literature, and language. The Russian word for "thank you", means "may God save you." To say goodbye to someone departing for a long absence, Russians use a word which means to ask forgiveness of one another. In the past believers were forbidden the Eucharist if unforgiveness existed toward another person. Thus, it was important to ensure accounts were settled if someone was going away for a long time. Most Russians use these words today without thinking of their origin.

From the Orthodox perspective, the Orthodox church is the church of the twelve apostles, dating to the time of Christ. The church of Rome went their own way. Protestants splintered from those who split. Schisms are not appreciated. Most of our years of ministry in Russia was exclusively among atheists. Trust was built, and suspicions overcome. When a Russian friend came to Christ, often his friends were interested. Yet typically when his friends and family learned that he was not Orthodox, barriers would go up. Parents feared brainwashing by a western sect. During this time, Russians seeking God went to the Orthodox church. Although today in Russia, seventy percent of the population identify themselves as Orthodox, priests tell me that only a very small number are practicing Orthodox - as few as 3% to 5%. They tell me that the task before them in the re-evangelization of Russia.

When I talk to Protestant Christians in Russia, some tell me that the Orthodox fight against them. A few tell me of immoral priests. When I talk to Orthodox believers, some tell me of immoral scandals among the Protestant missionaries and how the Protestants oppose them. Sadly, both are speaking the truth, but it is only a small part of the overall picture.

Overcoming Barriers

The foregoing paragraphs were written by me many years ago. The early nineties was a period of great spiritual interest in Russia and also of interest in the West as the figurative Iron Curtain was opening and a literal wall between East and West in Berlin was demolished. jDuring that period, it was unusual for me to be permitted to give public talks in Russia about the Bible. In 1989 a national deputy even invited me to give a series of lectures in Moscow at the City Hall of the Dzerzhinsky Region, where the headquarters of the secret police was located.

In the public school building of the residential area where I lived, I was given an opportunity to present the book of Romans, taking a chapter each evening. One evening at the beginning of the lecture a priest stood and interrupted me. "Why did you come to Russia?" he asked., "Do you think there is no Christianity in Russia?"

Some in the crowd tried to quiet him, but he refused to sit down. I answered, "For many years Christians in America have been praying for believers here. Now that it is possible to travel here openly, everyone excitedly has come rushing in. We haven't always been very wise. I have no intention to harm the church. I only want to help." With that he let me continue.

Afterwards I invited him to my apartment, which was in a neighboring building, and he reluctantly agreed. Once inside my home, I suggested we read and discuss a chapter from one of the Gospels. I placed an icon on my bookshelf, crossed myself and asked him to pray. We had a very warm and encouraging discussion of the passage we read. After that, we stood and faced the icon again as he prayed. I wasn't prepared for what came next. He embraced me and kissed me in the Russian custom. He asked if we could meet again. He explained that he never expected such a meeting when I invited him, and it was something he needed. We continued to meet weekly.

Later he confided to me some difficulties that had arisen. He was being criticized for meeting with a Protestant. He would respond, "Steve crosses himself and prays before the icon." His critics replied, "Well, maybe it's OK then." Forms can be obstacles or bridges.

Another Russian friend Oleg once observed how Paul went to great extremes to not create barriers for the Gospel with his Jewish audience, even having his disciple Timothy get circumcised before traveling to Jerusalem. Oleg added that in his experience so few Protestants seemed willing even to cross themselves for the sake of reaching others without an unnecessary hindrance.

Ye Shall Know Them by Their Fruits (Not Their Forms)

Living in another culture, I became aware of how much I depended on external forms for discernment. When these externals were missing, I was at a loss. Jesus had said, "Do not judge by appearances, but judge with right judgment."[54]

My former church in Long Beach asked me to address a class of missionary candidates one summer during my visit to the United States. I described to the class the following scenario: "You attend a Bible study with some Russian believers, a heart-warming time. You sense oneness of one heart and mind as you discuss the Scriptures. At the end of the discussion, everyone stands and faces an icon, crosses themselves, and someone recites a prayer. As you sit down, the person next to you asks you who is your favorite saint while he pours you a small glass of vodka." Then I asked the class, "How would you answer him?"

Listening to their responses, I took note of which particular forms constituted an issue, a misunderstanding, or, for some, a stumbling block. The question arises, "How do you identify a genuine believer when the familiar forms of your culture are missing?"

Jesus told a story that I found helpful with this question. He described how shepherds would leave their sheep in a large corral with other sheep. When a particular shepherd returned to gather up his sheep, he simply called out to them. The sheep that belonged to him responded to his voice and came out from the herd. "To him the gatekeeper opens. The sheep hear his voice, and he calls his own sheep by name and leads them out. When he has brought out all his own, he goes before them, and the sheep

---

[54] John 7:24

follow him, for they know his voice. A stranger they will not follow..."[55] I'm not good at recognizing God's sheep in an unfamiliar setting, if at all. But when I open the Word of God with someone, and we discuss it together, I often experience that conversation becomes less superficial, openness and trust increases, and our deeper values surface. We either respond to truth, or we resist truth. The responsiveness can be an indicator. Jesus said, "My sheep hear my voice, and I know them, and they follow me."[56]

A realization that has overflowed from living and relating in another country is that these principles of discerning the kingdom apply in my own native culture as well. The comfortable, familiar external indicators that I have unconsciously used to recognize faith are not necessarily reliable signposts at all. By not judging others through the lenses of religious forms (wineskins). we may begin discovering outcroppings of the kingdom (wine) in the most unusual, surprising places!

---

[55] John 10:3-5

[56] John 10:27

"From that time Jesus began to preach, saying, "Repent, for the kingdom of heaven is at hand."[57]

―――――――――――

"The kingdom of heaven is like treasure hidden in a field, which a man found and covered up. Then in his joy he goes and sells all that he has and buys that field. Again, the kingdom of heaven is like a merchant in search of fine pearls, who, on finding one pearl of great value, went and sold all that he had and bought it."[58]

―――――――――――

"And this gospel of the kingdom will be proclaimed throughout the whole world as a testimony to all nations, and then the end will come."[59]

---

[57] Matt. 4:17

[58] Matt. 13:44-46

[59] Matt. 24:14

THUMP KEG PUBLISHING
ThumpKegPublishing.com

Comments are welcome and can be addressed to:

Steve Slater
1630 W Ridge St
Wytheville VA 24382

Email: thumpkeg@icloud.com

Blog: https://thumpkeg.blogspot.com

Sales: https://ThumpKegPublishing.com